Your Bridge to Conventions

An in-depth look at modern bridge conventions.

Weak Two Bids

D1412371

Bridge with Patty!

Bridge with **Patty!**

Foreword

When I began playing bridge in 1964 I read everything I could put my hands on about bridge. I read about conventions and theory. I read humorous accounts from the bridge table and even bridge biographies. Every aspect of bridge fascinated me. I couldn't learn enough. I wanted to know more. I probably only play a tenth of all the things I have learned and read but I don't begrudge one minute of the time I have spent devouring everything I could.

Having taught bridge for over thirty years I am always excited to find a bridge player with an insatiable desire to learn more about the game. I'm very involved in teaching young players. In previous years we gave the students copies of the Bridge Encyclopedia when they reached the status of Junior Master. One of the players who received a book came to class the next weekend and asked me, "So what do you think about Morton's Fork?" He was making his way through the Bridge Encyclopedia and had gotten all the way to the 'm's! Nothing is more fulfilling than finding a kindred spirit, others who love the game and want to learn more.

What I hope to do, for those of you who have that drive to learn, is to create a vehicle in this series of books that allows you to learn and practice the conventions and theories in which you are interested. Beginner, Intermediate and Advanced topics will all be addressed.

Remember that for every convention invented, bridge players have come along and created treatments, quirks and options that they think will improve the bid – I'm no different. I do, however, try to let you know when I deviate from the original and give you options as 'Additional Notes" of things you might like to try.

Enjoy, learn, practice and **never** stop feeding your desire for more bridge knowledge!

Patty Tucker
American Bridge Teachers Association Master Teacher
American Contract Bridge League Accredited Teacher
Better Bridge Accredited Teacher
2000 North American Open Pairs National Champion

Weak Two Bids

Weak Two Bids (Weak Two) are opening bids that fall outside the normal parameters which are used for one-level opening bids. Weak Two opening bids are used to describe hands with a good, long suit and little defensive value. In general these are considered "defensive bids". Bids designed to prohibit your opponents from describing their hands easily to each other.

A Weak Two can be an opening bid of 2♦, 2♥, or 2♠. An opening bid of 2♣ is **not** a Weak Two. We reserve 2♣ to show 21+ high card points (HCPs) hands or the equivalent in trick taking ability.

A Weak Two is always an opening bid which shows:

- A six-card suit;
- A good suit (generally two of the top three honors or three of the top five);
- 5-10 HCPs;
- Usually will not contain a four-card major; and
- Usually will not contain a void.

Some examples of a Weak Two Bid:

1) ♠AK9854 ♥82 ♦3 ♣Q642
   Six good spades and 9 HCPs.

2) ♠54 ♥AKJ982 ♦J73 ♣42
   Six good hearts and 9 HCPs.

3) ♠4 ♥82 ♦AQ9742 ♣Q642
   Six good diamonds and 8 HCPs.

4) ♠AJ10984 ♥82 ♦32 ♣K42
   Six good spades and 8 HCPs.

After opening a Weak Two, opener will not bid a second time unless forced to bid by responder. Responder's two forcing bids (a new suit and 2NT) are discussed later.

While responder and opener might occasionally have strong enough hands or good enough fits to make a game, these bids are primarily defensive bids. As such, responder will concentrate on the strategic value of his hand. Responder will be considering:

- How many trumps do we have?;

- What is partner's distribution?;
- How many tricks can we take if our long suit is trumps?;
- How many HCPs do we have between our two hands?;
- How many HCPs do the opponents hold?;
- What is the opponent's distribution?;
- How many tricks can we take if our long suit is not trumps?;
- Can the opponents make a game?; and
- What is the vulnerability?.

In some cases, responder will decide to bid high enough to take the contract away from your opponents even though he expects his contract will be defeated; knowing that the amount of points the opponents will score for setting him will be less than the points they would have scored if they had taken the contract for themselves. This is called a "sacrifice".

While some rules will be described in responding to your partner's bid, never forget that the focus will be about taking tricks, not counting points. A discussion of how to count tricks follows after responder's bidding structure.

NOTE: A Weak Two opening bid is not made by a fourth seat opener. If the first three players pass and you are in fourth seat an opening suit bid at the two level shows an 'intermediate' hand. An opening bid of 2♦, 2♥, or 2♠ would show a six-card suit, 11-15 HCPs and a willingness to consider game (expecting to make the contract) if responder has one or two tricks and a fit.

The hand might look like this:

♠AKQ854 ♥82 ♦3 ♣KQ42

Six very good spades, a second good suit, 14 HCPs. If responder has three spades and an Ace in any suit, the possibility for game is very good, even though we might not have 25-26 points between our two hands.

Responder's Bids

As opposed to responding to one-level opening bids, HCPs **are not** the most relevant consideration in responding to a Weak Two. Many of responder's bids will be strategic. **Responder must always consider the vulnerability in his decision** but, in general, responder will:

- Pass with any hand that does not contain at least at two-card fit containing at least one honor;
- Raise to the three-level with any balanced hand with a three-card fit;
- Raise to the four level with any three-card fit containing a singleton or void; and
- Raise to the four-level with any four-card fit.

On the rare occasion responder has a good hand (16+ HCPs) **and** a fit with opener:

- If the opening bid was 2♥ or 2♠, the most likely game will be in four of partner's major suit; or
- If the opening bid was 2♦, the most likely game will be in 3NT.

Generally, responder should not expect that he and partner could make a game unless he has a fit with opener's suit and can count enough tricks to make game.

On hands that responder is considering game but feels more information would be helpful in making his decision, responder has two forcing bids available. They are:

- A new suit; and
- A bid of 2NT.

A new suit is forcing for one round and is most often used when the Weak Two opening bid was 2♦ and responder has a major suit. To choose the option of bidding a new suit responder would have a hand that holds something like this:

1) ♠AKQ84 ♥2 ♦Q63 ♣A642
   Five very good spades and 9 HCPs.

2) ♠54 ♥AKJ982 ♦J73 ♣42
   Six good hearts and 9 HCPs.

3) ♠AJ10984 ♥82 ♦32 ♣K42
   Six good spades and 8 HCPs.

> If opener has three card support or two-card support and one of the top three honors for responder's suit; opener will raise one level regardless of his high card point strength. ***Remember, after having opened a Weak Two, opener's strength is already established***.
>
> If opener cannot support responder's suit he will:
>
> - Rebid to his six-card suit at the lowest level; or

- Bid a second four-card suit if he has one.

Remember, bidding a new suit forces the Weak Two opener to bid again. If you do not have a fit for opener's original suit, bidding a new suit may commit you to a level where you are unable to make a contract.

A bid of 2NT (called a "feature bid") says nothing about the distribution of responder's hand, it simply asks opener a question – Do you have an Ace or King outside of your long suit? This bid is usually used when responder has a fit with partner and a relatively strong hand but is still not sure if game is likely. Responder's hand might look something like this after opener has bid a weak 2♥ bid:

4) ♠A84 ♥K432 ♦63 ♣AQ42

Responder can envision that their partnership probably has six heart tricks, one spade trick and one (or two) club tricks for a total of 8-9 tricks. If opener has the ♣K, responder can count 10 tricks and will bid game in hearts. If opener has the ♠K, responder can count 9 tricks and if the club finesse works 10 tricks, therefore, opener will bid game in hearts. If opener shows either the ♦A or ♦K, opener can count 8, 9 or 10 tricks depending on whether opener has the ace or king of diamonds and whether or not the club finesse works and will not bid game as it is unlikely to make.

Opener's response to the 2NT bid is easy:

- If opener has an Ace or King outside of his suit, opener will bid the suit that contains that card at the three level; and
- If opener does not have an Ace or King outside of his suit, opener will return to his six-card suit at the lowest level.

Responder will use the information elicited by each of these bids to place the contract at the appropriate level in the appropriate contract.

How to count tricks (not points).

Learning how to count tricks (not points) is an acquired skill. From the bidding alone, you have to imagine what cards your partner's hand contains and the distribution of his/her hand. That information has to be extrapolated to what the opponents' hands might look like and their likely contract and result.

A quick example:

Let's imagine that your partner opens a Weak Two bid of 2♥ showing six hearts with a good suit.

I would envision that partner's hand looked something like this:

♠42 ♥AQ9872 ♦942 ♣52

My hand is:

♠7 ♥K643 ♦AK6 ♣87643

I wouldn't know exactly what partner held in real life but if partner's hand is what I envision, what suppositions could I make? I would think that:

- The opponents have a good spade fit;
- The opponents have about 24 points;
- The opponents will be short in hearts (in fact I know that one of the opponents has one or zero hearts);

- The opponents have only two or three losers between their two hands if spades are trumps; , and
- Our partnership has nine tricks if hearts are trumps (six hearts, two diamonds and trumping one spade in the hand that holds four hearts).

Even if the opponents have not bid as yet, all of those suppositions would lead me to expect that they will bid. That they will bid spades. That they can and make and will bid a game in spades. These same suppositions would bring me to the conclusion that I should try and take the bid away from our opponents, *regardless of the number of high card points my partner and I hold.*

I should bid 4♥ in an attempt to win the auction for my side. If the opponents bid 4♠, I should consider the vulnerability to decide whether or not bidding 5♥ would be an acceptable sacrifice.

Vulnerabilty Factors

As responder to a Weak Two Bids be cognizant of:

- The vulnerability;

- The opponent's expected score if they make their contract; and
- Your expected loss if you win the bid, they double you and you go down.

Here is a brief example of the profit or loss of competitive bidding at the game level.

If responder's opponents bid and make a game they get:

Vulnerable 600+ points Non-Vulnerable 400+ points.

If responder bids higher than the opponents' game, they double you for penalty and you go down the opponents will get:

Number of Tricks Set	Vulnerable Doubled	Non-Vulnerable Doubled
-1	200	100
-2	500	300
-3	800	500
-4	1100	800

Notice that if responder is Vulnerable he should be much more cautious than Non-Vulnerable. Even though the opponents sometimes forget to double, responder should always base his decision expecting to be doubled.

Weak Two Bids

Board 1

North Deals
None Vul

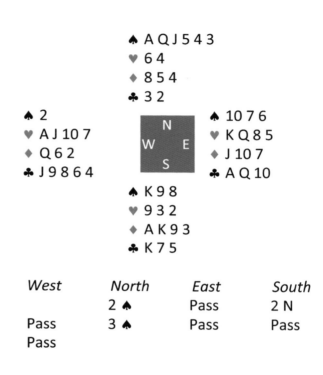

	♠ A Q J 5 4 3	
	♥ 6 4	
	♦ 8 5 4	
	♣ 3 2	

♠ A Q J 5 4 3
♥ 6 4
♦ 8 5 4
♣ 3 2

♠ 2
♥ A J 10 7
♦ Q 6 2
♣ J 9 8 6 4

♠ 10 7 6
♥ K Q 8 5
♦ J 10 7
♣ A Q 10

♠ K 9 8
♥ 9 3 2
♦ A K 9 3
♣ K 7 5

West	North	East	South
	2 ♠	Pass	2 N
Pass	3 ♠	Pass	Pass
Pass			

2♠ = A Weak Two Bid showing a six-card spade suit with two of the top three honors or three of the top five honors and 5-10 HCPs.

2N = An artificial bid asking partner if they had an Ace or King (a feature) outside of the spade suit.

3♠ = I have no outside A or K.

Weak Two Bids

Board 2
East Deals
N-S Vul

```
              ♠ K Q 6 4 3
              ♥ 10 9
              ♦ 9 3
              ♣ Q 6 4 2
♠ A 10 9                      ♠ 7 2
♥ Q J 7 5          N          ♥ 8 6 2
♦ K 8 7        W      E       ♦ A Q J 10 6 4
♣ A K 3            S          ♣ 10 9
              ♠ J 8 5
              ♥ A K 4 3
              ♦ 5 2
              ♣ J 8 7 5
```

West	North	East	South
		2 ♦	Pass
3 N	Pass	Pass	Pass

2♦ = A six-card diamond suit with two of the top three honors or three of the top five honors and 5-10 HCPs.

3NT = I would like to play game. I think I can take 9 tricks. My tricks would be six diamonds, one spade and two clubs. *Remember, if your long suit is a minor, ask yourself if it is possible to play NT as it is generally easier to take nine tricks than eleven tricks.*

Weak Two Bids

Board 3
South Deals
E-W Vul

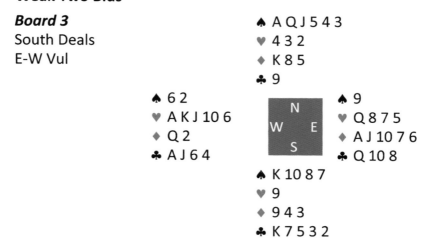

	♠ A Q J 5 4 3	
	♥ 4 3 2	
	♦ K 8 5	
	♣ 9	
♠ 6 2		♠ 9
♥ A K J 10 6		♥ Q 8 7 5
♦ Q 2		♦ A J 10 7 6
♣ A J 6 4		♣ Q 10 8
	♠ K 10 8 7	
	♥ 9	
	♦ 9 4 3	
	♣ K 7 5 3 2	

West	North	East	South
			2 ♠
Pass	4 ♠	Pass	Pass
Pass			

2♠ = A Weak Two Bid showing a six-card spade suit with two of the top three honors or three of the top five honors and 5-10 HCPs.

4♠ = With a good spade fit and a weak hand, South jumps to game. *Remember, when you have a good fit for partner's suit it is sometimes to your advantage to bid to a high level immediately and make it difficult for the opponents to bid, even though you are fairly certain you will go down.*

As you can see E/W can make 6♥, but the will be unlikely to enter the auction

Weak Two Bids

Board 4
West Deals
Both Vul

♠ Q J 10 9 8
♥ J 7
♦ J 5
♣ K 10 8 3

♠ K 6
♥ 9 6 3
♦ A Q 9 8 6 4
♣ 9 4

	N	
W		E
	S	

♠ 7
♥ A K Q 8 5 4
♦ K 7 3
♣ Q 6 5

♠ A 5 4 3 2
♥ 10 2
♦ 10 2
♣ A J 7 2

West	North	East	South
2 ♦	Pass	2 ♥	Pass
3 ♥	Pass	4 ♥	Pass
Pass	Pass		

2♦ = A Weak Two Bid showing a six-card diamond suit with two of the top three honors or three of the top five honors and 5-10 HCPs.

2♥ = A natural bid showing a good six-card suit or a self-sufficient (solid) five-card suit, with the values in either HPC or tricks to consider game likely and forcing opener to bid. ***Remember a new suit by responder is forcing one round.***

3♥ = I have either three hearts or two hearts with an honor.

4♥ = Since you have a heart fit I think we can make game in hearts.

Weak Two Bids
Board 5
North Deals
N-S Vul

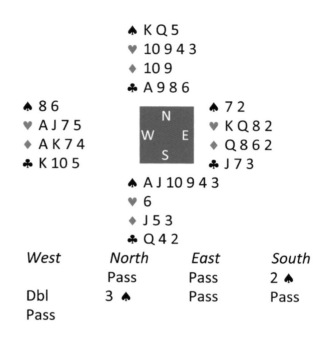

		♠ K Q 5	
		♥ 10 9 4 3	
		♦ 10 9	
		♣ A 9 8 6	

♠ 8 6
♥ A J 7 5
♦ A K 7 4
♣ K 10 5

♠ 7 2
♥ K Q 8 2
♦ Q 8 6 2
♣ J 7 3

♠ A J 10 9 4 3
♥ 6
♦ J 5 3
♣ Q 4 2

West	North	East	South
	Pass	Pass	2 ♠
Dbl	3 ♠	Pass	Pass
Pass			

2♠ = A Weak Two Bid showing a six-card spade suit, with two of the top three honors or three of the top five honors and 5-10 HCPs.

3♠ = With three trumps you would, generally, raise partner to the three-level as a strategic bid, hoping to keep East silent.

Weak Two Bids

Board 6
East Deals
E-W Vul

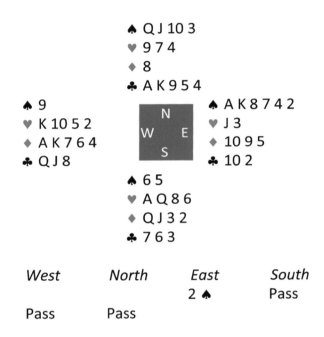

	♠ Q J 10 3	
	♥ 9 7 4	
	♦ 8	
	♣ A K 9 5 4	

♠ 9		♠ A K 8 7 4 2
♥ K 10 5 2		♥ J 3
♦ A K 7 6 4		♦ 10 9 5
♣ Q J 8		♣ 10 2

	♠ 6 5	
	♥ A Q 8 6	
	♦ Q J 3 2	
	♣ 7 6 3	

West	North	East	South
		2 ♠	Pass
Pass	Pass		

2♠ = A Weak Two Bid showing a six-card spade suit with two of the top three honors or three of the top five honors and 5-10 HCPs.

Pass = I believe we should play 2♠. *Remember, if you do not have a fit with partner's suit, it is unlikely that you can make any game regardless of the number of high card points you hold.*

Weak Two Bids

Board 7

South Deals
Both Vul

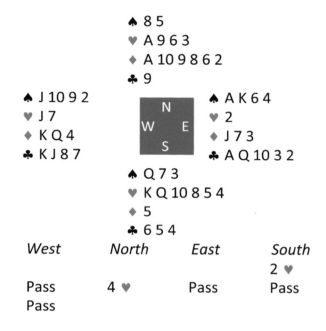

	North	East	South
West	*North*	*East*	*South*
			2 ♥
Pass	4 ♥	Pass	Pass
Pass			

2♥ = A Weak Two Bid showing a six-card heart suit with two of the top three honors or three of the top five honors and 5-10 HCPs.

4♥ = With a weak hand and a good fit, North raises to game. This is a strategic bid made in the hopes that E/W will pass and allow N/S to keep the bid. North is unconcerned that, if they play 4 ♥, they will not make their contract.

Weak Two Bids

Weak Two Bids

Board 8

West Deals
None Vul

```
                    ♠ K J 9
                    ♥ 7 4
                    ♦ 10 8 7 5
                    ♣ K 7 3 2
    ♠ 6 3                        ♠ 10 8 5
    ♥ A J 10 8 6 3        N      ♥ K 9 2
    ♦ K J 9 2         W       E  ♦ A Q 6 3
    ♣ 10                  S      ♣ A 6 5
                    ♠ A Q 7 4 2
                    ♥ Q 5
                    ♦ 4
                    ♣ Q J 9 8 4
```

West	North	East	South
2 ♥	Pass	2 N	Pass
3 ♦	Pass	4 ♥	Pass
Pass	Pass		

2♥ = A Weak Two Bid showing a six-card heart suit with two of the top three honors or three of the top five honors and 5-10 HCPs.

2NT = Asking opener if they have an ace or king in another suit.

3♦ = I have the ♦A or ♦K.

4♥ = Since you have the ♦K (East holds the ♦A so knows that West is showing the ♦K), I believe we can take ten tricks. Six hearts, three diamonds and one club.

About the Author

Patty Tucker

Patty learned to play bridge in 1964 at the age of eleven and became a full-time bridge teacher in 1999. A familiar face at regional and national tournaments, Patty received national recognition upon winning the 2000 North American Open Pairs National Championship with long-time partner and husband, Kevin Collins. From Patty, "I teach for the immense satisfaction I get in passing on to others my love for the game of bridge".

Major Accomplishments:

- Georgia Bridge Hall of Fame (2012)
- ACBL Goodwill Member of the Year (2011)
- North American Open Pairs Champion (2000)
- National Goodwill Committee (ACBL)
- Sportsman of the Year, Unit 114 (2000)
- Emerald Life Master
- District 7 Goodwill Member
- National Goodwill Committee (ACBL)
- Unit 114 Recorder
- ACBL Certified Director
- ACBL Accredited Teacher
- American Bridge Teachers Association Master Teacher
- Better Bridge Accredited Teacher
- Co-Founder Whirlwind Bridge
- ACBL Youth Coordinator (May 2008 through December 2009)
- Trustee, Foundation for the Preservation and Advancement of Bridge (FPAB)
- ACBL National Charity Committee

24535111R00016

Made in the USA
Charleston, SC
27 November 2013